Next Time You See the
MOON

BY EMILY MORGAN

nsta kids
National Science Teaching Association
Arlington, Virginia

nsta kids
National Science Teaching Association

Claire Reinburg, Director
Wendy Rubin, Managing Editor
Andrew Cooke, Senior Editor
Amanda O'Brien, Associate Editor
Amy America, Book Acquisitions Coordinator

ART AND DESIGN
Will Thomas Jr., Director

PRINTING AND PRODUCTION
Colton Gigot, Senior Production Manager

NATIONAL SCIENCE TEACHERS ASSOCIATION
David L. Evans, Executive Director
David Beacom, Publisher

1840 Wilson Blvd., Arlington, VA 22201
www.nsta.org/store
For customer service inquiries, please call 800-277-5300.

Lexile® measure: 940L

A Year of Moon Phases: 2015 (pp. 24–25) copyright ©2014 by W.L. Bohlayer, Celestial Products/MoonCalendar.com
Special thanks to Dean Regas, outreach astronomer at the Cincinnati Observatory Center, for reviewing this manuscript.

NSTA is committed to publishing material that promotes the best in inquiry-based science education. However, conditions of actual use may vary, and the safety procedures and practices described in this book are intended to serve only as a guide. Additional precautionary measures may be required. NSTA and the authors do not warrant or represent that the procedures and practices in this book meet any safety code or standard of federal, state, or local regulations. NSTA and the authors disclaim any liability for personal injury or damage to property arising out of or relating to the use of this book, including any of the recommendations, instructions, or materials contained therein.

Library of Congress Cataloging-in-Publication Data
Morgan, Emily R. (Emily Rachel), 1973- author.
  Next time you see the moon / by Emily Morgan.
      pages cm
  Summary: "This book inspires children to observe the Moon. Readers will learn how the Moon's changing shape is caused by its orbit around the Earth."-- Provided by publisher.
  Audience: K to grade 3.
  ISBN 978-1-938946-49-3 (library edition) -- ISBN 978-1-938946-33-2 -- ISBN 978-1-938946-55-4 (e-book) 1. Moon--Juvenile literature. I. Title.
  QB582.M67 2014
  523.3--dc23
                              2014018065
Cataloging-in-Publication Data are also available from the Library of Congress for the e-book.

To my dear friend Jenni Davis, for sharing the wonders of the sky with me and countless others.

"In every walk with Nature
one receives far more than he seeks."
— John Muir

A Note to Parents and Teachers

The books in this series are intended to be read with a child *after* he has had some experience with the featured objects or phenomena. For example, go outside on a clear night, lie on a blanket together, and stare up at the Moon. You can find moonrise and moonset times for your area online. Talk about what you observe and what you wonder. Share how you feel as you lie on the Earth and look up at the sky. Over the next few weeks, pay attention to the Moon's changing shape as the days pass. Notice that sometimes you can see the Moon at night, and sometimes you see it during the day. You might even keep a record of the changing shapes on a calendar and record your observations and questions in a Moon journal.

Then, after you've had some experiences observing this beautiful satellite of ours, read this book together. Take time to pause and share your learnings and wonderings with each other. You will find that new learnings often lead to more questions.

The *Next Time You See* books are not meant to present facts to be memorized. They were written to inspire a sense of wonder about ordinary objects or phenomena and foster a desire to learn more about the natural world. Children are naturally fascinated by the Moon, and when they learn that its changing shape is caused by its orbit around Earth, the Moon becomes even more remarkable. My wish is that after reading this book, you and your child feel a sense of wonder the next time you see the Moon.

—Emily Morgan

Next time you see the Moon, look carefully for a few minutes. How would you describe its shape? Does it look like a glowing circle, a tiny sliver of light, or something in between? Have you ever recognized a pattern to the Moon's changing appearance?

The Moon's beauty and changing shape have inspired art, music, poetry, and storytelling throughout history. Have you ever wondered why the Moon appears to have different shapes at different times of the month?

Because of its orbit!

The Moon's *orbit* is the path the Moon follows as it travels around Earth. The Moon's different shapes, or *phases*, have to do with its particular location in this orbit.

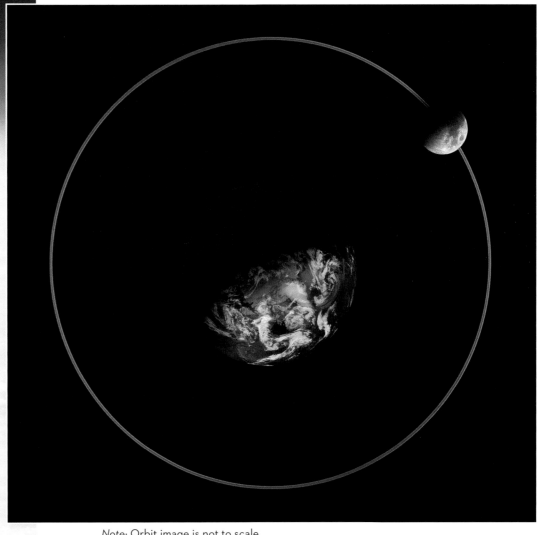

Note: Orbit image is not to scale.

The Moon makes no light of its own. It reflects the light of the Sun.

So does Earth, and all of the other planets, too.

Half of the Moon is always lit by the Sun, but when that lighted side faces away from Earth, we can't see the Moon at all. We call that phase *new Moon*. As the Moon orbits Earth, a few days later we can begin to see a tiny sliver of the lighted side, a *crescent Moon*.

As the Moon continues on its path around Earth, day after day we see more of the part that reflects sunlight. When we can see half of the lighted side, we call this a *first quarter Moon*.

When the Moon's place in its orbit allows us to see more than half of the lighted side but not quite the whole thing, that is called a *gibbous Moon.*

Several days later, we can see the entire lighted side of the Moon, a beautiful *full Moon.*

As the Moon continues in its orbit, we begin to see less of the side that's reflecting sunlight. We see a gibbous Moon again, but this time the light is on the opposite side of the Moon.

The gibbous Moon is followed by the *last quarter* Moon.

A few days later, we can expect to see another crescent Moon. After that, we are back to new Moon, and then the cycle begins again.

If you keep track of the Moon phases for a while, you will discover that it takes about a month (actually, a little more than 29 days) to observe all of the Moon phases. This is because it takes about a month for the Moon to orbit the Earth. So, when you look at the Moon today, know that you will see that same phase again about a month from now.

The phases of the Moon always occur in the same order. In the days after a new Moon, we see more and more of the lighted side. We say the Moon is *waxing*, which means growing. Of course, the Moon is not *actually* growing; we are just seeing more of the lighted side as the Moon orbits Earth.

New Moon   Waxing Crescent   First Quarter   Waxing Gibbous   Fu

After a full Moon, we begin to see less of the lighted side. We say the Moon is *waning*, which means shrinking. We see less and less of the lighted side until we are back to new Moon, and the cycle begins again. All of these changes happen because the Moon is orbiting Earth.

Moon   Waning Gibbous   Last Quarter   Waning Crescent   New Moon

A Year of Moon Phases

	Thu 1	Fri 2	Sat 3	Sun 4	Mon 5	Tue 6	Wed 7	Thu 8	Fri 9	Sat 10	Sun 11	Mon 12	Tue 13	Wed 14	Thu 15	Fri 16	Sat 17
January					FULL												

	Sun 1	Mon 2	Tue 3	Wed 4	Thu 5	Fri 6	Sat 7	Sun 8	Mon 9	Tue 10	Wed 11	Thu 12	Fri 13	Sat 14	Sun 15	Mon 16	Tue 17
February			FULL														

	Sun 1	Mon 2	Tue 3	Wed 4	Thu 5	Fri 6	Sat 7	Sun 8	Mon 9	Tue 10	Wed 11	Thu 12	Fri 13	Sat 14	Sun 15	Mon 16	Tue 17
March					FULL												

	Wed 1	Thu 2	Fri 3	Sat 4	Sun 5	Mon 6	Tue 7	Wed 8	Thu 9	Fri 10	Sat 11	Sun 12	Mon 13	Tue 14	Wed 15	Thu 16	Fri 17
April				FULL													

	Fri 1	Sat 2	Sun 3	Mon 4	Tue 5	Wed 6	Thu 7	Fri 8	Sat 9	Sun 10	Mon 11	Tue 12	Wed 13	Thu 14	Fri 15	Sat 16	Sun 17
May				FULL													

	Mon 1	Tue 2	Wed 3	Thu 4	Fri 5	Sat 6	Sun 7	Mon 8	Tue 9	Wed 10	Thu 11	Fri 12	Sat 13	Sun 14	Mon 15	Tue 16	Wed 17
June		FULL														NEW	

	Wed 1	Thu 2	Fri 3	Sat 4	Sun 5	Mon 6	Tue 7	Wed 8	Thu 9	Fri 10	Sat 11	Sun 12	Mon 13	Tue 14	Wed 15	Thu 16	Fri 17
July		FULL														NEW	

	Sat 1	Sun 2	Mon 3	Tue 4	Wed 5	Thu 6	Fri 7	Sat 8	Sun 9	Mon 10	Tue 11	Wed 12	Thu 13	Fri 14	Sat 15	Sun 16	Mon 17
August														NEW			

	Tue 1	Wed 2	Thu 3	Fri 4	Sat 5	Sun 6	Mon 7	Tue 8	Wed 9	Thu 10	Fri 11	Sat 12	Sun 13	Mon 14	Tue 15	Wed 16	Thu 17
September													NEW				

	Thu 1	Fri 2	Sat 3	Sun 4	Mon 5	Tue 6	Wed 7	Thu 8	Fri 9	Sat 10	Sun 11	Mon 12	Tue 13	Wed 14	Thu 15	Fri 16	Sat 17
October													NEW				

	Sun 1	Mon 2	Tue 3	Wed 4	Thu 5	Fri 6	Sat 7	Sun 8	Mon 9	Tue 10	Wed 11	Thu 12	Fri 13	Sat 14	Sun 15	Mon 16	Tue 17
November											NEW						

	Tue 1	Wed 2	Thu 3	Fri 4	Sat 5	Sun 6	Mon 7	Tue 8	Wed 9	Thu 10	Fri 11	Sat 12	Sun 13	Mon 14	Tue 15	Wed 16	Thu 17
December											NEW						

CELESTIAL PRODUCTS™ A Year of Moon Phases: 2015. Copyright ©2014 by W.L. Bohlayer, Celestial Products / MoonCalendar.com

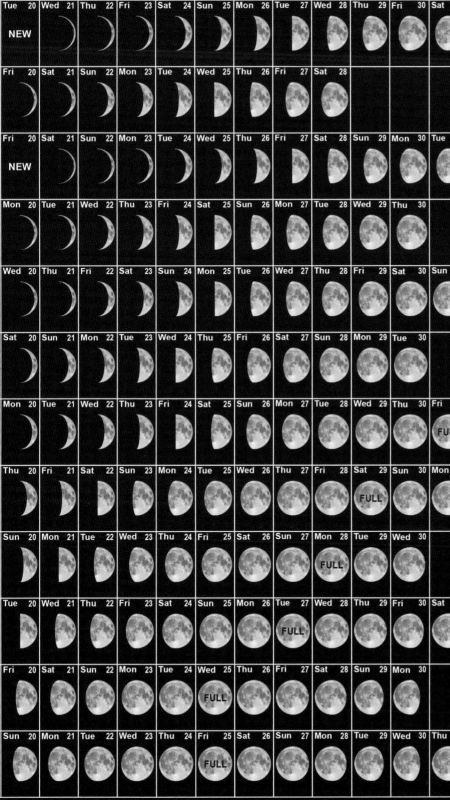

The Moon always orbits in the same direction and takes the same amount of time to circle Earth, so the phases of the Moon are regular and predictable. In fact, scientists know what the Moon phase will be on any given date— even thousands of years into the future Isn't that amazing?

When you see the Moon at night, it is definitely the brightest object in the dark sky, which is probably why we notice it more at night than during the day. But if you look carefully, you can see the Moon during the day quite often.

Because Earth is turning while the Moon is orbiting, moonrise and moonset times are different each day. Sometimes the Moon rises at night, and other times it rises during the day. One thing always remains the same: The Moon rises in the eastern sky and sets in the western sky, just like the Sun and stars, because Earth always turns in the same direction.

So, the next time you see the Moon, remember that the shape you see depends on where our Moon is in its orbit around Earth. Half of the Moon is always reflecting light from the Sun, and we can see different parts of that lighted side as the Moon travels around our planet. Isn't that remarkable?

About the Photos

Family under the Moon
(Tom Uhlman)

Boy pointing at the Moon
(Tom Uhlman)

Van Gogh's *Starry Night*
(Getty Images)

The Moon in orbit
(NASA)

The Moon in orbit
(Getty Images)

Moon and Earth
(NASA)

Crescent Moon
(Steven David Johnson)

First quarter Moon
(Judd Patterson)

Gibbous Moon
(NASA)

Full Moon
(Steven David Johnson)

Gibbous Moon
(NASA)

Last quarter Moon
(NASA)

Moon phases
(NASA)

Waning crescent
(Tom Uhlman)

Boys observing the Moon
(Tom Uhlman)

Moon phases
(NASA)

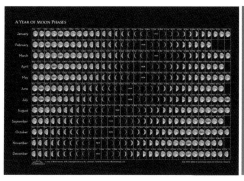

Moon phase calendar
(Mooncalendars.com)

Gibbous Moon
(Steven David Johnson)

Moon at sunset
(Judd Patterson)

Observing the Moon at night
(Tom Uhlman)

Moon model setup
(Steven David Johnson)

Moon model in action
(Steven David Johnson)

Activities to Encourage a Sense of Wonder About the Moon

❖ Use a model to help you understand how the Moon's orbit around Earth causes changing shapes. Use a lamp to represent the Sun and a smooth, opaque ball to represent the Moon. Your head will represent Earth. As you make the ball orbit your head, you will see different parts of the side of the ball that the lamp is lighting up (a).

❖ For example, when the ball is in this position in its orbit around your head, you can see a tiny sliver of the lighted side of the ball—a crescent Moon (b). Keep the ball orbiting your head so you can see it go through all of the Moon phases. A video of this Moon modeling activity can be found at *www.nsta.org/nexttime-moon*.

❖ Keep a Moon calendar by recording the shape of the Moon each day. Look for patterns and predict the next phase.

❖ Use NASA's Lunar Phase Simulator to move the Moon in its orbit and see what Moon phase we see on Earth.

❖ Use the Moon Connections "Moon Calendar" web tool to find out what Moon phase it will be on your next birthday or on your birthday 10 years from now, and compare the Moon phases that are seen in the Southern Hemisphere to those seen in the Northern Hemisphere.

Websites

NASA's Lunar Phase Simulator
http://astro.unl.edu/classaction/animations/lunarcycles/lunarapplet.html

Moon Connections "Moon Calendar"
www.moonconnection.com/moon_phases_calendar.phtml

Next Time You See series
www.nexttimeyousee.com

Downloadable classroom activities can be found at *www.nsta.org/nexttime-moon*.

*Note: The order of the Moon phases pictured in this book and the explanations shared apply to Earth's Northern Hemisphere.